Mr. Special Meets Leo

SHARON JENISE HALL

Mr. Special Meets Leo
Copyright © 2022 by Sharon Jenise Hall

ISBN
978-1-958122-96-9 (Paperback)
978-1-958122-97-6 (eBook)

Acknowledgments

This book is dedicated to Cheryle A. Lane, a.k.a. "Chief." Chief is appreciated and loved for her loyalty and dedication to our organization. After witnessing her love for her grandson Leo, an awesome two-year-old who was unable to write the letters of the alphabet, I became inspired. I thought if Leo could meet Mr. Special, he could help him learn. And guess what, he did! Chief can now present her grandson with his first personalized book. It features Leo and Mr. Special. Mr. Special teaches girls and boys how to show respect and how to demonstrate love. He also shows them how special they are. The book *Mr. Special Meets Leo* is a "special way" for Chief to say, "Grandson, I love you so much. I want you to succeed in life, and I pray God blesses you abundantly."

During the winter, Mr. Special was invited to Mrs. Precious Daycare Center for their class celebration.

Before the party started, the children were finishing
their parents' holiday cards and paintings.

When Mr. Special walked in, some of the children ran over to meet him. A couple of the children ran away because they were afraid while others kept on writing and painting.

However, there was one child who stood off and just stared at Mr. Special with the most amazingly bright big eyes.

This child caught Mr. Special's attention.

Mr. Special walked over and asked the child what is his name.

The child answered, "My name is Leo, and I am two years old."

He said, "Look at my card for my grandmother who lives in Georgia."

Mr. Special was amazed and surprised to hear a two-year-old
speak so clearly and state where his grandmother lives.

Now it was time to share with the class their paintings and who the holiday cards were for before wrapping them up.

All the children presented, and Leo wanted to be last.

He said he wanted to write his grandmother a letter to tell her how much he loved her and misses her, and then he said, "I do not know how to write the letters."

He also wanted to tell her that he could count up to twenty but do not know how to write the numbers either.

Mr. Special immediately went over to Leo and told him he would teach
him how to write the letters of the alphabet and the numbers.

a	am	an	and	can
do	for	go	has	have
he	here	I	in	is
it	like	look	me	my
no	play	said	see	she
so	the	to	up	we

Mr. Special also told him he would teach him how
to read some sight words as well.

Leo asked, "Will you really do that for me?"

Mr. Special said, "Yes."
That really put a big smile on Leo's face.

Now Mrs. Precious collected all the cards and paintings from the children.

Then the party began!

Leo said that he wanted to sit with Mr. Special, and he did!

All the other children said thank you to Mr. Special
for coming to their holiday party.

Mr. Special Meets Leo

Workbook

Letters of the Alphabet

A _____

_____

a _____

_____

B _____

_____

b _____

_____

C _____

_____

c _____

_____

D _____

_____

d _____

_____

E _____

_____

e _____

_____

F _____

_____

f _____

_____

G _____

_____

g _____

_____

H _____

_____

h _____

_____

I _____

_____

i _____

_____

J _____

_____

j _____

_____

K _____

_____

k _____

_____

L _____

_____

l _____

_____

M _____

_____

m _____

_____

N _____

_____

n _____

_____

O _____

_____

o _____

_____

P _____

_____

p _____

_____

Q _____

_____

q _____

_____

R _____

_____

r _____

_____

S _____

_____

s _____

_____

T _____

_____

t _____

_____

U _____

_____

u _____

_____

V _____

_____

v _____

_____

W _____

_____

w _____

_____

X _____

_____

x _____

_____

Y _____

_____

y _____

_____

Z _____

_____

z _____

_____

Numbers 0-20

0 _____

_____

1 _____

_____

2 _____

_____

3 _____

_____

4 _____

_____

5 _____

_____

6 _____

_____

7 _____

_____

8 _____

_____

9 _____

_____

10 _____

_____

11 _____

_____

12 _____

_____

13 _____

_____

14 _____

_____

15 _____

_____

16 _____

_____

17 _____

_____

18 _____

_____

19 _____

_____

20 _____

_____

Sight Words

I	go
see	down
the	my
you	do
can	put
me	like
and	said
we	of
on	come
to	have
was	

Color Words

red   brown

blue   black

green   white

yellow   purple

orange   pink

Rhyming Words Match

see	pie
you	bee
man	bake
rake	can
sky	blue

Number Words

zero	eleven
one	twelve
two	thirteen
three	fourteen
four	fifteen
five	sixteen
six	seventeen
seven	eighteen
eight	nineteen
nine	twenty
ten	

www.ingramcontent.com/pod-product-compliance
Lightning Source LLC
Chambersburg PA
CBHW041555120626
46551CB00002B/215